Everyone loves *Be True to Your School* and Bob Greene. . . .

"If Bob Greene's diary doesn't take you back to high school, you didn't go. But if you did, it doesn't matter when. You'll remember what it was like to be seventeen, to be happy, to be hurt, to fall in and out of love. It's a wonderful book."
                    Elmore Leonard

"Bob Greene's memoir of high school, 1964, provokes laughter, thought, and nostalgia, that residue of pleasure. What's so effective about this book is that whoever reads it will do just what I did: remember."   Rita Mae Brown

"Bob Greene is a national treasure, a writer who never misses anything funny or touching in the American character."
                    Dan Jenkins

"Bob Greene is a virtuoso of the things that bring journalism alive: Literary talent, hard reporting, a taste for mixing it up haunch-to-paunch, shank-to-flank, and elbow-to-rib with people of all sort   Tom Wolfe

(More)

*Published by Ballantine Books